THE SUPPOSED HUNTSMAN

THE SUPPOSED HUNTSMAN

BY

Katie Fowley

UGLY DUCKLING PRESSE

BROOKLYN, NY

2021

ISBN 978-1-946433-81-7
First Edition, First Printing, 2021

Ugly Duckling Presse
The Old American Can Factory
232 Third Street #E-303
Brooklyn, NY 11215
www.uglyducklingpresse.org

Distributed in the USA by SPD/Small Press Distribution
Distributed in the UK by Inpress Books

Artwork by Mollie Goldstrom
Design and typesetting by Doormouse
The type is Didot

Books printed offset and bound at McNaughton & Gunn
Cover offset by Prestige Printing
Covers printed letterpress at Ugly Duckling Presse

The publication of this book was made possible, in part, by a grant from the
National Endowment for the Arts, by public funds from the New York City
Department of Cultural Affairs in partnership with the City Council, and by
the continued support of the New York State Council on the Arts with the
support of Governor Andrew M. Cuomo and the New York State Legislature.
This project is supported by the Robert Rauschenberg Foundation.

CONTENTS

for Katie Taylor

They were afraid in the deep dark woods.
But luckily they found the joy of the heart.
The joy of the heart is little marks on the tree.

Red cause the house is red.
So they were safe enough.
And then Gretel went back to sleep.

But it's a different heart.
It's called the Elephant Heart.
Trail of red bits.

Then Gretel woke up.
She saw her parents.
She was so amazed.
She was just amazed.

The owl said, "Good God, they went away from me."
But everyone was so, so, so amazed.

— Paloma Dillon, age 3

I.

INITIATION

Sir Lizard threw a party.
Hibiscus, soaked.
Bed, soaked.
Scar spots to distinguish
one animal from the other.
Fire spots lighting up huts.
With resin, cook yams.
With poles, pole your way to the turtle.
What is so terrifying, turtle?
Don't walk away.
In my uninitiated state
> I confused a penis with a tail, a turtle with dark, a boy
> with a girl. They both wore white feathers. I stripped
> the feathers. I buried my face, half-dead. I nested in
> hibiscus. I was stripped and held. I was held and the
> teeth knocked out.

My name is turtle.
My house is dark.
Turn my body in the fire.
Dance all night to bring down dawn.

RECOGNITION

Before the event
a man ranks as woman.
Before the event
a woman ranks as man.
A man rank as woman
ranks a woman.
A woman rank as animal
ranks a man.
There are rank animals
in the shrubgrove
rank animals with vegetal
shields. Revolving shapes
sweep across the sandbeach.
Similar feathers, darker
falling to the beach.
To recognize you is to gift you.
What is it to beg?
A scarlet contusion
makes its way—
one, two, three
evolutions, one, two
three incisor teeth
of the large kangaroo.
This dance is for selection.
Shake your fist at it.
Shake your feather.
Solemnly pierce your ears.
      It is rank
      rank
      rank
      to shake

so violently.
Oh animal
cast in yellow
teeth of the animal
found in place.
I would recognize you
but you are so yellow.
I would recognize you
but you are so rank.

PARK

I was on Sheep Meadow, then the Great Lawn, then the
        Pine Cove.
I was on the pine floor
and it nettled me.
Desire nettled me
with wing-thin fingerlings
a feeling of the pretty
the sound of approach.

*

The desire to scrabble together
in time for the next showing.

Trouble with visualization.
How to love without possessing.

*

It's nice today
but there is sweat pant love, and I don't like that
and there's a German Shepherd
and I don't like that either.
There's a shimmer on the water
and it moves across.
I like it when ducks stick their tails in the air.

*

Choosing where to sit in the park—
Don't sit too close to single men.

They might take it as suggestion
power of.

*

Everything emotes.
These legs
kick you
the glancing breeze
this lighting.

*

How to find a direct emotion?

Tap it at the root.

Sordid root.

WHAT IS SEX?

Is it maintenance?
Is it deliberate?
Is it appropriate?
What is this sexual creature in socks?
Is it molting?
Does it change?

Where is the white cat that sought sunlight?

The frigid air.
The vanquished cat.
The giddy hawk.
The unkempt cat.
The upset hawk.
The unwed cat.
The hawkish dog.
The rusty cat.

What is sex?
Is it unbelievable?
Is it second hand?
Would you prefer it with wool?
A terrible interest.

Were I with you, were I with you—

If it doesn't pour out of you
a wider net.

SIMPLETON

The gatherers of simples
hole up in the bush.

You stupid goose,
everything is again consumed!

Over and over
I fell upon my neck.

I was loathsome and unwashed
but happily I found The Joy

of the Heart and it radiated out
a simple medicine served up.

We lived in a sweat, combustible.
We lived in Simpleton for a while

where simple apples grow
and single arrows shoot

eternally. I'm dirty
but who gives?

Our house is not hard.
Simple enough.

I come to a big piece of water.
How do I cross?

COLD DANCE

It is cold as green horses
And it is cold as custard
Is cold.

The cold hand creeps.

It is cold as waking and it is cold as blisters.
The street is cold.

Our appetites are cold.
Often it is cold.
Harden in the cold
Looking at the cold Buddha.

The cold dogs climb up
Climb up
Climb up
From cold.

The cold makes
Your face animate.

The cats are fed but cold.
There is heat in your belly.

The city starts to creep
Starts to creep
With cold.
It is warm in places of commerce
Then cold.
It is warm as finance

And it is warm as language
And we sit here talking about cold.

See me straddling the cold.
See me smiling like a fox.

FORCED DANCE

I can't force this horse.
Dance damn horse.
You can't curse out a horse.
Dance dry horse.
I can't dance like a swan.
This swan is half-gone.
Feed this swan.
I can't muster a must.
Dance damn dust.
This dust isn't lush.
We'll make it lush.
Not with a brush.
Not with a brush!
    Hand me a spoon and a molting pot.
    Hand me a beat and spigot of rot.
    Hand me a bell and a halting buck.
    Hand me a saddle. Hand me a rock.
    Hand me a train, cradled in thought.
    Hand me a hunter who'll
Hunt me till dusk.
Can you dance with a hunter?
You can dance well enough.
You can wind.
You can swell.
And you roll like a clop.

AUSTERE MEASURES

I.

I will taste my mouth.

What's austere?
A seer.
An oyster full of hairs.

Master of the Leaping Figures,
may I leap with you?

You may not leap.

Master, I long to tear the silk.

You may not tear it.

I run the better to taste my salt.
I run out of rope.

You may not leap
into your office.

I have no office
of which to speak
not a window
not a sink.

Master, I long to taste the milk.
Master, may I feel your throat?

If it comes to this.
If we cut the bush.

Master, may I pick a rose?

You may not smell it.

II.

Are you satisfied, Brother Dog?

Yes, with flesh.

Are you satisfied, Brother?

Yes, but I want to know.

Are you satisfied, cloth?

Yes, but I shiver.

Are you satisfied, spinner?

I am satisfied, but I have not touched the bread.

III.

Austere seagulls ball up on Brighton Beach.
It is winter.

The frost we steer to
and the frost we steel ourselves to
and the frost we see to

and the frost we move to.

I come to a breach
the tide all tangled up
in grasses, weeds,
a churning place.

Master, it grows cold and ugly.

Take this salt.
It will leave you hungry.

SIMPLETON

I am mute as a fish and not a word escapes me.
Not a word escapes me and my wanting arm.
I am mute as fruit and nothing holds me.

I run after you hotly.
Not a word escapes.

I was dull when I went out.
I held my plate before my eyes
and cried it wet.
Then all was green.
Then came the flowers.
Then all the trees
made me light and happy.

How horribly you look.
I run after you hotly.
So hot I am lost
in the forest
and will not sing.

I jump in numb water
and burn open like a bird.

I have lost my senses
walking in the sea.

I sing for nothing
underneath the almonds
of the almond tree.

GRAVITY

In my house-like costume I inhabit space.

This is a grave business.
What is this grave business?

I came dressed as plumbing
and you came dressed as plumbing too.
Childhood is so intensely serious.

What are we doing
in our crinolines
in states of undress?

Paint the body
with symbolic patterns.

What is a symbolic pattern?
What color for mourning?
What color for moving on?

Red, black, pale yellow, red.

Twirling satisfaction, plumage, deviation —
Spin fast as your monster cage will allow.

PARK

Bark at my back.
A tree is a porous thing.
I keep expecting animals.
Shade makes green things plusher.
Exposed skin, purpling plants.

I watch the biker in a state of stretching
impolite to stare but possibly more allowable here in
        the park
to stare and to talk
like the fat man who was talking to the woman in her
        underwear.
He was so forward under the tree.
Her love scent followed her
a scent to luxuriate in like a damp cloth.

The stretcher stretched then left.
Light dusts through air.
Where does one wash clothes?

TERRIBLE

I am not able.
Terrible as a truck full of chickens.
Terrible as a sun-bent ripple.
Terrible nipple.

I'm in a state.
The news is terrible.
Hardly a thought has begun
before all thoughts are terrible.

I have a terrible stain on my shirt.
This food is terrible.
Ten terrible looking dogs bound over
with their ten terrible mouths
and their hunger.

On the rocks by the river, a couple puts its arms
around each other. Terribly public
and terrible ardor. I am terribly long
like a building. I touch the terrible skyline
with my terrible sandal tan. It is terrible to see
the sun go. This is not my boat
my sunless boat. These are not
my dogs, my black, stout dogs.
These are not my shoes, these are everyone's shoes
and the shoes of every child
in a terrible heap of trash
on a terrible island
in a terrible park
possible to enter.

You look terrible.
And your heart looks too.
And the gleaming sewage treatment plant
lights up its tumid orbs. And the creek,
waxing noxious, floats an armada.
A shimmering armada shakes sand from its sails
every grain of it terrible as glass.

SIMPLETON

I am going to Simpleton to find something better
      than death.
If I make music, it will have full play.

For anything I know is stolen.
For anything I know falls in the kettle
is devoured by the hungry dog.

I am traveling to find something better.
To find something better, the bird refuses to work.

For anything I know is fast upon me.
For anything gusts.
For anything moves in the throat.

I am traveling to find a better dog.
I am traveling to find the antidote.
I am traveling to learn how to shiver.

For anything I know, I long to be there.
For anything I know, I am a scholar.

Make me into soup for the morrow.
I will suit myself to the times.

II.

PARK

I abort all plans
and lie down in the park.
Seeded weeds course through.
The dark is always the giddiest.

I remove my shine and lie down in the park
like a graying tendril
that thins as it starts.
I remove all bristles
and lie down. No one cleans
in the dark park. No one weaves
in utmost dark.

How did you get so dark, park?
You have a gleam and a thought
a wind pushing trees apart. In the dark
lovers exchange letters.
I dress with feathers.

I know an animal
that gives off sparks.
I know a tree that's yellow now.

THE TELLER

I charge the banks.
I hit a groove
and it is winter
in my country.

I go to the teller.
The teller gives me a temporary card.
It is dusk between us.
I speak through tablets
that touch me without reaching for my hands.

The teller does not touch me.
He is tall like an endangered plane tree.

The teller was raised in the mountains
drinking mountain tea.

The teller migrates like fashion.
He speaks to me through glass.

He tells without thinking,
tucks his shirt in,
tells and tells like a fungus that spreads
irreverently, without end.

Teller, if you trust me, tell me.
Tell it straight until it ends me.
Teller, if you love me, tell me.
Tell the whole company.

Tell me where to go from here.

I am a wave.

When the teller kisses me, I turn into a company.

Gentlemen don't kiss and tell.
I'm not a gentleman.
I'm a branch in a current of money.

Tie me to that tree.
Tell me another current will wash us.
Tell me it's only temporary.

DUET

my destitute
with arms with
apples
horns or
sticks my
glimmer not
glib but dancing
in central park
to a dance
of your own
notation once in
september when I
did not
love

my doublet
my coarse
self my
dull flesh
dented
into shape

we dance in
the living
room
in this
world mostly

LAP DANCE

You make my soul wet.
There are holes in it and the cork shows through.
You make me wet enough to celebrate.
You make me wet enough to come
and then you make me contemplate.

You make me wet in my non-parts.
You make me wet below my map of the Antarctic Peninsula.
I'm coming down in the Metropolitan Museum.
What was the big event?

I am dry as peat.
I am half asleep.
I am barely humid.
My brow is loose.

You make my soul leak.
What to do with all these wet spots?

You stall the furniture
And I am sated to my bed.

You make the moon wet.
No, it is gilded there.

You make me base.
You make me basic.
You make me complicated.

You make me pour
oil into oil.

You make my soul lap.
You make me constant as rain.

Lover of plastics and pallets
lay me out on a pallet.
I will be this blue.
Feed me dinner and then dinner.
I will eat all my dinners.
I am wide like the moon.

EMU

Who is that dark emu drifting in my neighbor's coat?

Emu and the horse of thoughtless feeling.
Silly, faceless bird emoting.

Emu, I welcome you
to my yard of wet blossoms.
Emu, I write for your tongue.

Emu of green deliberations,
damp feathers and a swampy head.

Emu of art.
Emu of misgiving.
Emu simmering in warmer climes.

Emu, dry your tears on this tissue.
How your face folds in ultimate grief.

Propulsive emu.
Joy without sound.
Emu in the green, herbal air.

Emu, groaning under its weight
under a great weight of emu,
a plurality of emu
and a sick sun.

Emu, I wish you decadence and rest.
Be with me

in personal dusk,
humming felon that you are.

Can I quote you, emu?
By nature without flight.
Loose cipher with stout legs.

Emu, aspiring to be something other than emu,
aspiring to be ultra-emu,
to be more than dead weight.

Back-to-the-land emu.
Remunerated emu
with a coin on your tongue.

Emu of denuded continents,
spirit me away
in a ghastly breeze.

*

I'll be sorry to see
your meat on the menu.

Emu, my cousin, and the tongues of the church.
Emu and the molten dawn.

Emu of fluid gender.
Emu of fluid tongue.

Emu, your silky head.
Bed death, breath nest.
Friendship lands on you like a gnat.
Emu of a thousand apologies
malingering in a blue lagoon.

Emu dressed to the nines,
dressed to kill me in my sleep.
Sweet emu with agitated eyes,
the naked neck, the flesh.

I don't want this literal, low-calorie emu.
Don't want it.
Won't have it.
Won't abide.

Skinny emu in a glut of emu.
Overpopulating emu gunned down.

General emu, marching to his death,
hilarious, headless, obese.

Your intolerable sadness.
Your wings are a vestige.

Emu of vocables,
emu of faltering breath—

Color me with your emu eyes,
your private, loping emu eyes.

BLUE TRAIL

I woke up like this
in a field.
I woke up like this
in the wet sun.
I was conscious of a field.
My thoughts began to run.

I woke up in the mud of color
sensitive fog
blue as shelter.

*

I see the ground hog in its hole.
If it grows much larger, it will fill up its hole.
This far north, vigilantes swoop.
There are many ways to be a poet, lover, scholar.
Gray is not so bad for green.
I hear your voice and mist.

No dark but the woods are dark.
No dark in the portrait.

*

Trees form another country.
Trees offer shade
to a mind less shady.

They get on like a house on fire.
They get on like water.

*

The animals may arrest you
in the path.

The fast ants form
their crumple nests.

I'm excited to see you
in the meadow
to show you the meadow

uncontained
harboring harbors.

*

I call to you and only half of you.
I call to you like certain grass.
I call you and you are picking strawberries, or about to.
I call to you and your basket of fruit.
I call to you sadly.
I call to you, and only half a man responds.

RESTITUTION

Because a sleeping buffalo
To get a voice out of a head
Because a father died
There are two fathers dead
Collect needles
And make a pine
Collect bones
And make a face
It was human song that pulled him from the dust
It was human hair
It is the virtue of the buffalo to wallow
And so the cliffs are lined with buffalo but none of them
      will jump
There is no tension in the herd
It stretches out and blurs
      The fawn is lost
      The field is fickle
      The wind is soft
      The brine is ripe
      The word is love
      The feeling fallow
      I feel a furrow
      Move my pelt. I
Pace slowly. The sky waits for me.
There's food to find and face the sheet. The wind is
      climbing
Over the lake.

TWELVE BROTHERS

My brothers are turned inside out.
My brothers are turned
with the snap of a lily.

Do you suffer?
Seven years dumb in the trees.
Seven years without laughter.

Nothing could be more proper
than to give the boys a pleasure.

Nothing could be more proper
than to roll her in the river.

Do you suffer?
Give us some.

I haven't got enough myself
so how can I give it?

Every time I speak
a toad pops out.

King, King, what are you doing?
What are you doing, King?

It's a drag—this gloomy forest
with no middle.

Wake up, King.
Am I not wonderful?

My looks make the animals afraid.

In the middle, the blood flows.
I don my cloak of paper.

Fall on my neck.
Fall in the thistles.

ROGUE

Every animal is deadly
even the shape-shifter.
The rogue animal sprints into the swamp, into the meadow,
    into the breeze.

On the island, a rogue white horse
ran across my field of vision.
He eyed me.

A decomposing pheasant wing
a fresh start.

The rogue-master has stripped my belief
has stripped the ponds.
The silent, brain-eating amoeba.

My best thoughts are rogue thoughts.
My best thoughts are sad.

I have a roguish wish
the voices of neighbors already risen, the children.

I've left behind my vision
am bald as an ant.

I have a roguish faith
a herd of miniature donkeys.

I have come to a standstill
somewhere furred and visual.

TEACHER-CREATURE

This is your teacher-creature speaking.
Hello blue jays, twits, and squirrels.
Hello black cat, orange, tabby.
The coffees of the world build a towering cappuccino
one day with winter stupor.

Teacher-creature thinks a little.
Teacher-creature amuses herself, writes an email, overhears
       students discussing their sex lives in the bathroom.
Teacher-creature suffers an appetite.
Teacher-creature studies socks and rare shades of bathrobe,
       studies acorns and plastic raindrops, studies backyard
       wildlife, the ways of semi-feral cats, warm rockets, the
       hollow sounds of hollow birds, studies lamb kebabs
       and other desired foods, studies desire, a Halloween
       nurse dripping from the leg...

This is your teacher-creature speaking in a sad month.
This is a creative brain, a Caliban.
This is supple sadness and a hundred of his friends.

This is your teacher-creature with a marked-down
       Valentine's balloon.
This is your teacher-creature flickering with faint instincts.

A student suspects you.
If my teacher is a creature, then who is this?
I am bereft as sweaty bath slippers, as the robust bird, as
       the lost carpet, as the stomach.

Evidence of the creature:
She arrives silently in the shower.
She is 20% brighter than oxygen.

What was it you wanted to see?
Everyone else had smoother feet and bones.

This is your teacher-creature
neither deep nor salty.
This is a loose head.
This is a creature, smelling of teeth.
This is a teacher, unnaturally healthy.
This is a high order of creature sent to sea
so we might begin to see her smart.

HOT DANCE

I am putting on a hot mask.
I am lying in the hot grass.
I am pushing open hot glass
Doors for you. I am drinking
From a hot flask. I am
Climbing up a hot mast to jump
Into the ocean. I am blowing
Through a hot brass
Instrument. Hot brass, hot
Brass, hiccup your burning
Tune. I am breathing hot
Gasps. I am loosening my hot
Dress. I am cooking up a hot mess
Of soup for you.
I'm a hot mess.
You're a hot mess.
We're a hot
Monsoon. I am thinking fast as hot
Air. I am feeling every hot hair
On my arm. I make a hot stain
Everywhere I go. Lava flows
Around me. Animals bask
Beside me. I let down
My hot locks I
Harvest some hot
Crops I climb over
Hot rocks. The heat
Pines, bristles
To talk.

THE SUPPOSED HUNTSMAN

Suppose I am a huntsman.
Suppose I am possessed by a lion.
Suppose I am rude and disoriented at my wedding.
Suppose I like to hunt.

Suppose I possess a lion.
Suppose the light is dappled.
Suppose I lose my face in the water.
Suppose I am not careful with my hands.

Suppose I desire water.
Suppose I foreclose in a shady arbor.
Suppose I am really myself
with a head full of brains.

Suppose the flies cough
in flashes of sensuality.
Suppose these are my legs.

Suppose I am an ever-available spring.
Suppose I generate feelings.
Suppose a dog stops to listen.

Suppose a lion possesses itself.
Suppose a lion possesses 6 out of 7 deadly sins.
Suppose my sin is the deadliest.
Suppose I drip with masculinity.

Suppose I believe in a larger wedding.
Suppose I believe in rapid heat.

In figure and stature
I resemble a hammer.
In figure and stature
I could be a king.

III.

SALT BATH

I feel like writing in my high-fertility poetry suit
The feeling of hair underwater
The feeling of feeling
My ancestor the onion
Dry onions in the mouth
Ancestral onion, time spent alone and salty
What is delightful about a thinking creature?
Creature thinks: So full of salt
I could levitate
I am going to know things
What dull grape
What looming tongue

PERFECT

Katie and I cleaned together.
Perfect.

The sheepshearers came today
Perfect.

And in the morning
the milk was perfect.

A woman of the cloth.
Perfect.
Fell into her cloth.
Perfect.

The animal stink
perfects the animal.

Katie and I slept.
Perfect.
In a perfect blue dress.
I went after her hands.
Perfect.

The animated hand.

The rain gathered up.
And the path was
too perfect to stop.

I went after the cows.
Perfect.

I went after Comfort, the horse.

I fixed my love buttons.
I fixed them again.

I woke up like this.
In the hard rain.

Was getting wetter at the pump.

Katie and I fucked each other.
Perfect.
Considering all the things that bite.

I took the tucks out of my skirt.
Sounded pretty.
Perfect.

Enchanted girls in a bark box.
Perfect.
Made a bonnet out of black lace.

She calls herself a huntress,
dons male apparel
and adopts an inner life.

LAST DANCE, or
THE FESTIVAL OF ST. JOHN

Turn a cart wheel and it follows you.
Gather cowslip and it clings to you.

I turn into a dancer.
I turn into a bear, longing
for a maiden in a tree.

St. John, so, so
Brisk and cheerful

When the river floods, we ride on rafts
over the city gates.

Is it the blood of the river that you leap so high?
Is it the heat of the fire that you leap so high?

After great leaping, one man lies weeping
St. John's name in his mouth.

Turn a corner and it meets you—

beasts and the footprints of beasts
breaths and the prints they left

a healthier plant and a hunger
a quiet came under.

GRAY DANCE

for Heidi

All cats are gray.
Even the orange cat turns gray.
Even the violet cat is gray.

I have pistols under my frock coat.
Even the sea looks gray.
When the candlesticks begin to talk
All coats turn gray.
Gray—another broken color.
All eyes are gray.
Getting grayer and grayer
And elder and elder.
All brows are gray.
The gray water snakes
Engender each other.
All snakes are gray.
Gray-moldering apples
Succumb to each other.
All fruit is gray.

In my goose-gray suit
I give birth to new weather.
All thoughts are gray.
Gray, the ambassador and gray, the lynx.
All muffled sounds are gray.
When all candles are out
In an ambient dusk
Unbutton your boots
And return to the South.

The snow appears gray
Against your white boots.
The bordering town is barely lit up.

I have a gray cat.
I have a gray coat.
When all candles are out
All candles are out.

LUFF OF MUSGRAFFE

Daunce a reil
Daunce a jig
Daunce a reil
Low-thing.

For luff of Musgraffe
Fulis me up
The muss in the hair
And the muss in the dusk.

Daunce a jig
Daunce a reil
Daunce a jig
Low-thing.

For luff of Musgraffe
Fulis me up
The salt in the water
And the salt in the crust.

Daunce a jig
Low-thing
Daunce a jig
Low-thing.

Like a fish in a bucket
Like a lake in a cup.

Daunce, luff, daunce
For luff, low-thing.
Fulis me up.

Fulis me up.

Bring me to water
And bring me a cup.

Daunce a reil
Daunce a reil
And fulis me up.
Wither you go
I come back up.

I HAPPEN WITH YOU

I am half above the hills.
I am half below my form.
My hands are full of roots and I have
disenchanted all the birds.

Come with me, wind through a fir tree.
Come skim the air like leaves.
Come to a place where the trees are more lofty.

I'd trade my gold dress
to spend one night in your chamber.
I would like to see you spread
on the hills like clover.

Into the blue water
I will go first
and fleece the clouds
with a fine-toothed comb.

EXPLICIT

Come rest
in the greenhouse
by the lemon tree. We'll eat
someone's science experiment.
My head will burn its energy. A fleet
of ships will meet me strung
between two coasts. Chase me
down a natural slope. My best joke
isn't really a joke.

CLEAN MIND

Bristles of leg
scuffed homage.

Having an idea —
Why do I want to have it?

Having hinders.
Having halters.

Half the idea falls
together after

but to be present
in a quiet body

there must be some pulse
funneling outwards

and dirt is already
making its way out of nails.

Then I think of carpenter ants
the sun too direct

it causes shifting
as when, as on

the morning bus left
and I with it.

A hot room without mold.
I have room for it.

I have movement
and it brings me here.

CROWN

I would like to crown you with this beauty.
A thing of beauty is a felon.
A felon takes me out.
I would like to crown you with a thing-like beauty
Beneath the molting tree.
I would like to crown you until you are wealthy
And somber enough to eat.
My haunches turn to rubber,
My crown of honey—complete.
A nimble quake. A quiver.
The passage opens with healthy ships
Envenomed in a fetid mist.
   A joyful felon stops and starts
   To keep the briny ghost afloat.

HAPPINESS

I am never more happy.

I am never more loose—
my swimming tongue,

I ate all the petals
in shades of orange and pink.

You lead me to a bower and bid me drink.
There, I reproduce morning.

In shades of roaring
our ears press against the lake.

My flag is wet.
I'm up to my ears in a lagoon.

Without region
the horse bounds.

I am never more happy
than when I hear the waves rock.

The rock feeling its grain.

I am never more happy
than when the moon jars me.

My soft production
the fatal sun.

MARY WOULD NOT

And the next day?

Mary would not.

And the third day?

Mary would not.

At the carwash?

Mary would not.

And on Saturday?

Mary would not.

Come with me, Mary, and sit upon my bushy tail.

Mary would not.

She would not migrate.
She stood planted
to the voluptuous ground.

Mary would not quit this life.
Mary would not marry.

She conceived a great love.
She microdosed on holy basil
and plunged into the pond.

Mary would not count her blessings.
Mary dressed in Viking garb and ran into the wood.

Mary would not sweep the sugar palace.
Mary swarmed.
Mary stung.

Mary ululated like a wood thrush.
She would not be muted.
She materialized.

BROTHER LUSTIG

for Farnoosh

Brother Lustig sits lustily on her haunches
eating her ammunition loaf.

She eyes the crumbs where they fall,
the creeping sun.

Brother Lustig flushes her poem down the toilet,
     accidentally.

She pulls herself clumsily onto the dock,
pulls herself through shades of sexuality,
writes sexts to the wind.

She begins to see everything as her lover.
Hey, fire extinguisher, looking good.
Hey, sexy table.

My brother, my long lost brother.
The cleavage of my brother is remarkable.
If I write about my brother's cleavage, will she mind?

It cleaves her white swimsuit,
the boob that escaped in Cuba when she nearly drowned
and was rescued by teenage boys.

Brother Lustig delicately shoos a mosquito from her coffee
without harm.

Brother Lustig consents to a two year contract as my
     brother.
My ecstatic brother, tripping on strong coffee and allergy
     pills,
tripping on wildness, upturned roots.

Brother Lustig holds my paw, bandages my wounded
     finger—
A brother like no other.
She's my kind of brother.

Brother Lustig laughs a great, deep belly-laugh that fills the
     house like a private joke.

Brother Lustig takes my hand and pulls me into the swamp.

Brother Lustig dreams of a detachable penis that ejaculates
     everywhere.

Brother Lustig clogs the toilet with pages of poetry.
     Literally.

Brother of early spring.
Brother of devotion.
Brother tumbling like a saint.

Everything I've said about my brother is true.
Everything I've said about my brother is real life.

My brother is a bit of a bro.
That's partly what I love about her.
When I love, the words tumble like the Jugglers of God.

I could write all day about my brother.

My brother likes her coffee strong.
Whatever you do, do not dilute her.

I become hungry and little bells go off.
It's like loosening a tap.

My brother cuts my pill in half
(a pharmacist's daughter).

My brother researches snails and waits for news of her
      father.

I am ready.
I am ready to receive my brother,

my mind filled with brotherly sentiment
"the banging bottom of the actual wind."

LULLABY

Let's all become nurses
And sleep in low places
A spa of red flowers
A block of old trees

Away from your window
Across from your building
A building like yours
Lets off its new steam

It's better this weather
It's better than silk

The sky is a gray thing
The sky wants to hold you
The sky is away now
It cannot white out

Let's all become nursemaids
And sleep in low places
Let's all become jelly
In a spa of red hearts

The heart is an urchin
The heart isn't well now
The heart has a fever
It wants to black out

Let's all become nurses
And sleep by the fire

The winter umbrellas
A host of red hair

It's a good thing this building
This mantle of gleaming
I'll build you a building
If you live there with me

Like snakes in the building
Like birds in the building
The men in the building
Are circling free

The dusk is a low thing
The dusk wants to hold you
You cannot be held now
You cannot walk out

Come out of your building
Fluorescent in gloaming
The windows are darkening
The smell of green tea

This green is depressing
This green light is fetching
The light from the ether
The light from your knee

Acknowledgments

Thank you to the editors of the following publications in which some of these poems first appeared: *6x6*, *Columbia Journal*, *Cosmonaut's Avenue*, *Dusie*, *FENCE*, *Poems by Sunday*, and *Swaddled with Ease*. Special thanks to Camilo Roldán, who first published some of these poems in the chapbook *Dances & Parks*.

I am grateful for the thoughtful attention of Daniel Owen, Kyra Simone, Matvei Yankelevich, and the rest of Ugly Duckling Presse.

Mount Lebanon Residency and Saltonstall Foundation gave me the time and space to complete this book. Thank you to Sarah Steadman, Evan Thaler-Null, and Lesley Williamson for their support and generosity.

Friends offered invaluable feedback and championed this book into existence. Thank you to Sara Deniz Akant, Rawaan Alkhatib, Ashley Colley, Callie Garnett, Taso Karnazes, Jessica Laser, Erica Dawn Lyle, Daniel Poppick, Adrienne Raphel, Heidi Ratanavanich, Colby Sommerville, and Bridget Talone. I am forever grateful to my teachers who sheparded me into poetry, from my teenage years to the present, particularly Patricia Smith, Stephanie Burt, and Lisa Jarnot. Special thanks to my parents for supporting my inclination towards poetry from a young age and driving me to poetry slams at the Cantab Lounge.

Thank you to Mollie Goldstrom for all the years of friendship and for the beautiful cover.

Deepest gratitude to Farnoosh Fathi, Michael McCanne, and Katie Taylor who made writing this book possible.